Civic Heroes: Discovering Elections with the Supervisor of Elections

An Exciting Journey into the World of Voting

Written by Alisa L. Grace

Illustrations by naqsa_art

This Book is Dedicated to:

To our future voters, we desire that children learn about civics and the voting process in a fun and engaging manner. We are committed to engaging them in learning about civics and the vital role of all parties involved in ensuring the success of our voting process.

Dear Parents and Teachers,

We are excited to share our new book, "Civic Heroes: Discovering Elections with the Supervisor of Elections," designed specifically for children aged 6-9. This book introduces young readers to the concepts of civics and voting in an engaging and age-appropriate way. We believe it's never too early to start teaching children the importance of being active and informed community members.

Why This Book is Important:

1. Foundational Knowledge: By learning about elections, voting, and the roles of various people involved, children gain foundational knowledge that will help them understand how their community and government work. This early exposure helps build a sense of civic duty and responsibility.

2. Critical Thinking: The book encourages children to think critically about their choices and understand their impact on their community. It fosters a sense of empowerment, showing them that even small actions, like voting, can make a big difference..

3. Engagement and Curiosity: The book captures the interest of young readers with engaging illustrations and simple explanations. It encourages them to ask questions and discuss what they've learned with their families and peers, promoting a lifelong interest in being active citizens.

4. Values and Responsibility: Teaching children about voting and civics helps instill important values such as fairness, responsibility, and community participation. These values are essential for their development as thoughtful and responsible individuals.

5. Parental and Educator Involvement: The book provides a wonderful opportunity for parents and teachers to discuss these important topics with children. It can be a starting point for meaningful conversations about how our communities function and each person's role in improving them.

We hope that "Civic Heroes: Discovering Elections with the Supervisor of Elections" will be a valuable tool in your efforts to educate and inspire the young minds in your care. Together, we can help children understand the power of their voices and the importance of their participation in the democratic process.

Thank you for your support and for helping shape our community's future voters and leaders.

Sincerely,
Alisa L. Grace

Introduction

"Welcome, Future Voters!"

Hello, kids!

Have you ever wondered how decisions are made in your town or school? That's where civics comes in! Civics is how community people work together to make rules and choose leaders. It's important because it helps everyone understand how to be good citizens and improve the community.

One way people participate in civics is through elections. Elections are special days when people vote to choose their leaders. These leaders make important decisions that help the community run smoothly. When you vote, you pick the person you think will do the best job. Every vote is important because it helps decide who will lead and make good choices for everyone. Even though you might be young, learning about elections shows how everyone can make a difference in making the community a better place to live!

VOTE

Civics
Elections
Vote

Vocabulary: Elections, vote, civics

2

Chapter 1

Meet the Supervisor of Elections

VOTE

"The Leader of the Voting Team: The Supervisor of Elections"

The Supervisor of Elections is like the team captain for voting! A supervisor is a person who is in charge and makes sure everything is done right. They have a big responsibility, which means they have a very important job and must take it seriously. They organize and oversee elections. To oversee means to watch over and make sure things are going well. This means they set up places where people can vote, ensure the voting is fair, and count all the votes to see who wins. The Supervisor of Elections helps everyone in the community have a chance to vote and choose their leaders. It's a very important job because it helps make sure our community is a good place for everyone!

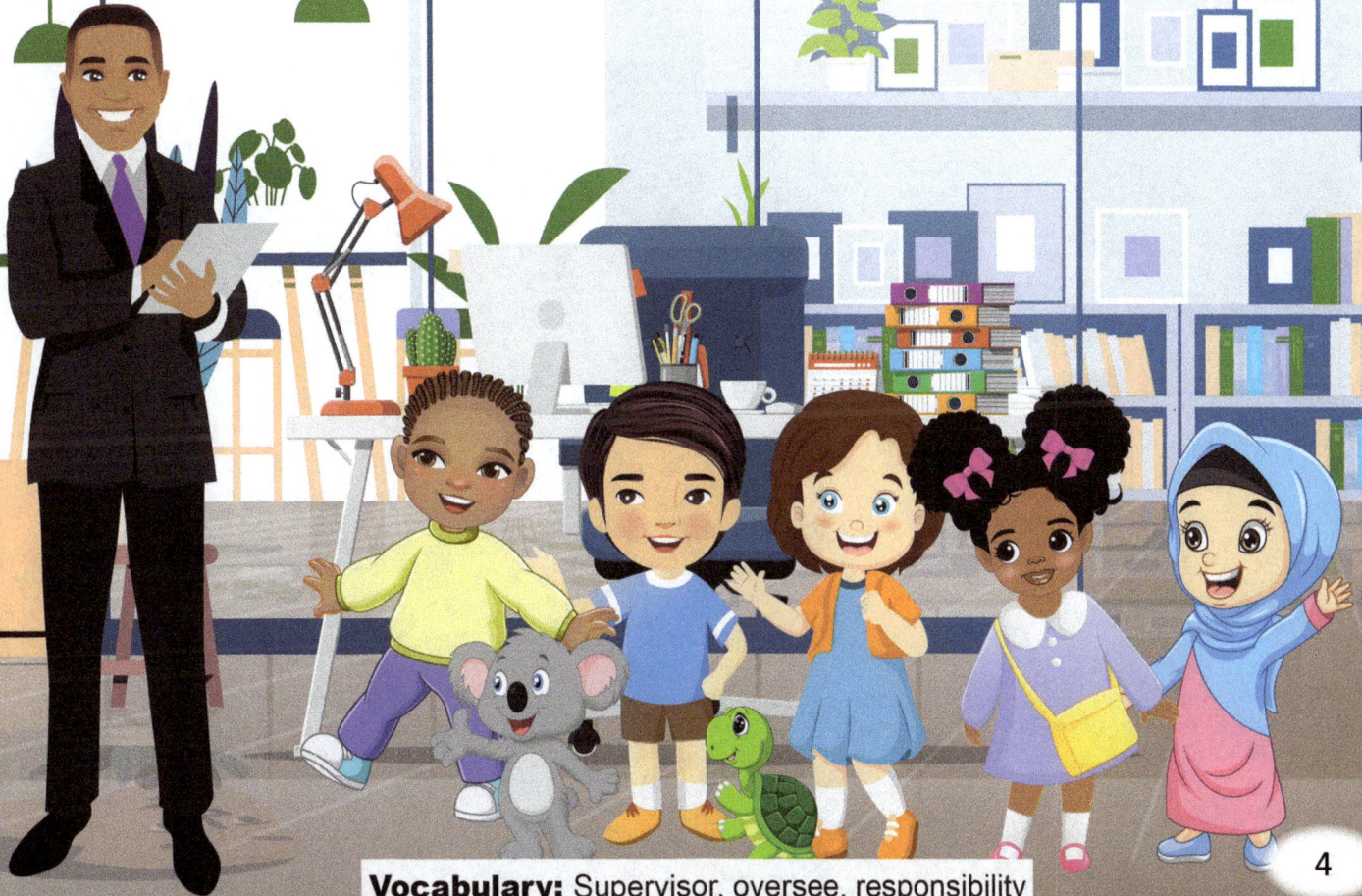

Vocabulary: Supervisor, oversee, responsibility

4

Chapter 2

Departments and Their Roles

VOTE

"Signing Up: The Voter Registration Department"

The Voter Registration Department is where people sign up to vote. To register means to sign up and put your name on a list. When someone wants to be a voter, they must fill out a voter registration form. This form asks for things like your name and address. You are registered to vote once you fill out the form and send it in! Registering is important because it ensures you can vote and help choose the leaders in your community. It's like joining a team that helps make important decisions!

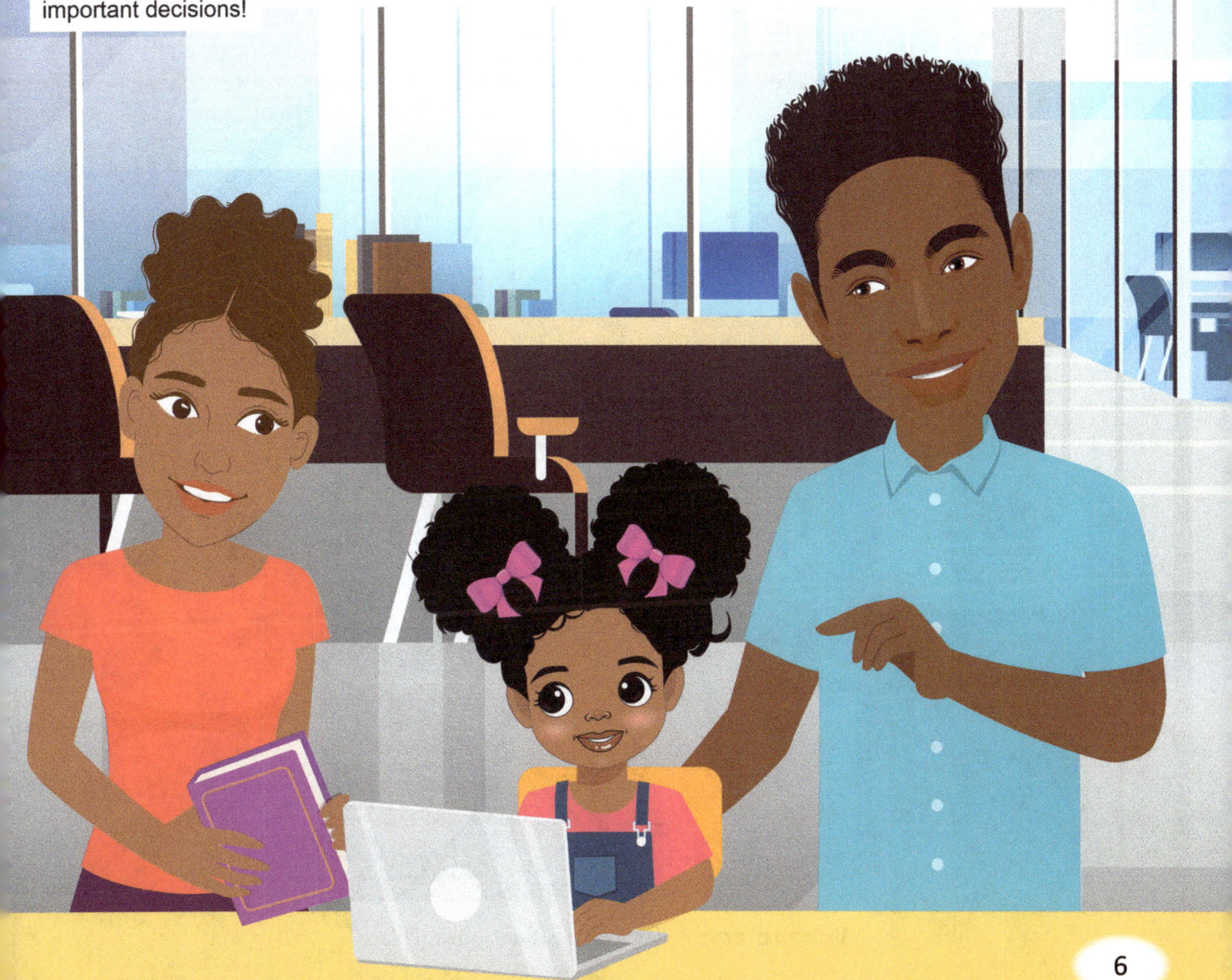

"Helpers on Election Day: The Poll Worker Department"

On Election Day, there are special helpers called poll workers. A poll worker is like an assistant, someone who helps. They work at the polling place, which is the location where people go to vote. Poll workers have many important jobs, like helping people find where to vote, giving out ballots, and ensuring everyone follows the rules.Poll workers are very important because they make sure everything runs smoothly and everyone has a chance to vote. WithouT them, election day wouldn't work as well!

VOTE

BALLOT BOX

Vocabulary: Poll worker, assistant, polling place

"Tools of the Trade: The Election Equipment Department"

People use special machines and tools to vote on Election Day, which are called election equipment. One important piece of equipment is the ballot box. A ballot is a piece of paper where you mark your choices, and the ballot box is where you put it when you're done. There are also special voting machines that help people vote by touching a screen or pressing buttons. These machines make voting easy and help count the votes quickly. All this equipment is very important because it ensures that voting is fair and everyone's vote is counted correctly!

VOTE

Vocabulary: Ballot, voting machine, election equipment, ballot box

"Spreading the Word: The Outreach Department"

The Outreach Department has a special job of helping people learn about voting. Outreach means reaching out to people and sharing important information. They go into the community, a group living in the same area, to inform everyone about how and why they should vote. To inform means to teach or tell people about something important. The Outreach Department might visit schools, make posters, or hold events to ensure everyone knows about elections and why it's important to vote. They help make sure everyone in the community has a chance to be part of choosing our leaders!

Go for vote

YOUR VOTE MATTERS

Vocabulary: Outreach, community, inform

Chapter 3

The Voting Process

VOTE

"Step-by-Step Voting"

Let's learn step-by-step what happens on Election Day! First, you go to the polling place, which is the location where people go to vote. When you arrive, you check in and get a ballot. A ballot is a paper where you mark your choices for who you want to be a leader. After you fill out your ballot, you go to a special box or machine to cast a vote. Casting a vote means turning in your ballot so it can be counted. Then, you're done! Your vote helps decide who will make important decisions in your community. It's a very exciting and important process!

Vocabulary: Polling place, ballot, cast a vote.

Chapter 4

Counting the Votes

VOTE

"How Votes Are Counted"

After everyone has voted, it's time to count the votes. To count means to add up all the votes to see how many each person got. Once all the votes are counted, we find out the results. The results tell us who got the most votes and will be the new leader. The person with the most votes is called the winner. It's very important that the counting is done carefully and fairly so that everyone's vote is included. This way, we ensure the right person is chosen to help make good decisions for our community!

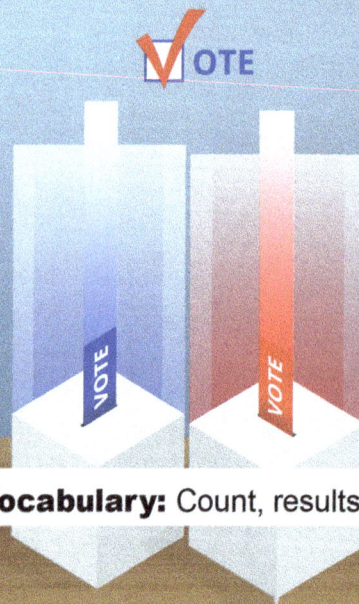

Vocabulary: Count, results, winner

Chapter 5

Why Voting Matters

VOTE

"Making a Difference: Why Voting Matters"

Voting is very important because it has a big impact on our community. Impact means it can change or affect things in a big way. When people participate in voting, they help choose the leaders who will make important decisions for everyone. A decision is when you pick what to do about something. By voting, everyone helps decide who will make rules and plans to improve our community. That's why everyone needs to vote – each vote helps shape our future and ensures everyone's voice is heard!

15

Vocabulary: Impact, participate, decision

Conclusion

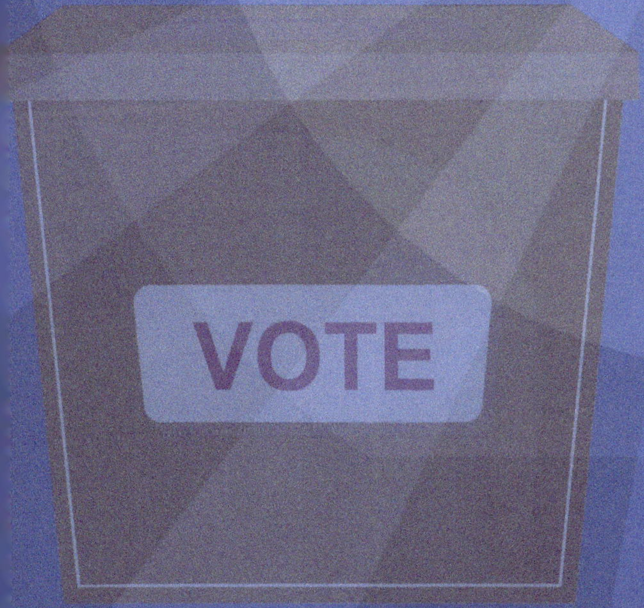

"Be a Voting Hero!"

Civics is important because it helps us understand how to be good citizens and improve our community. Voting is a big part of civics. When people vote, they help choose leaders who make important decisions that affect everyone. You can be a voting hero by talking to your family about voting and why it matters. Even though you might not be able to vote yet, you can look forward to participating when you grow up. Every vote makes a difference; you can help improve your community by participating in it!

Glossary
"Important Words to Know"

Here are some important words we've learned about voting and civics:

Elections: Special days when people in a community choose their leaders.

Vote: When you pick the person you think will do the best job.

Community: A group of people living in the same area.

Supervisor: A person in charge who ensures everything is done right.

Oversee: To watch over and make sure things are going well.

Responsibility: A job that is very important and needs to be taken seriously.

Register: To sign up and put your name on a list.

Voter: A person who votes in elections.

VOTE

Form: A paper with questions that you answer.

Poll worker: A helper on election day who assists at the polling place.

Assistant: Someone who helps out.

Polling place: The location where people go to vote.

Ballot: A piece of paper where you mark your choices.

Voting machine: A special computer that helps people vote.

Equipment: The machines and tools used during voting.

Outreach: Reaching out to people and sharing important information.

Inform: To teach or tell people about something important.

Count: To add up all the votes.

Results: The total votes that show who won.

Winner: The person with the most votes.

Impact: To change or affect things in a big way.

Participate: To take part in something.

Decision: When you pick what to do about something.

These words help us understand how voting works and why it's important for everyone in the community!

VOTE

The Supervisor of Elections

VOTE

VOTE

R

D

ELECTION

E PLURIBUS UNUM

22

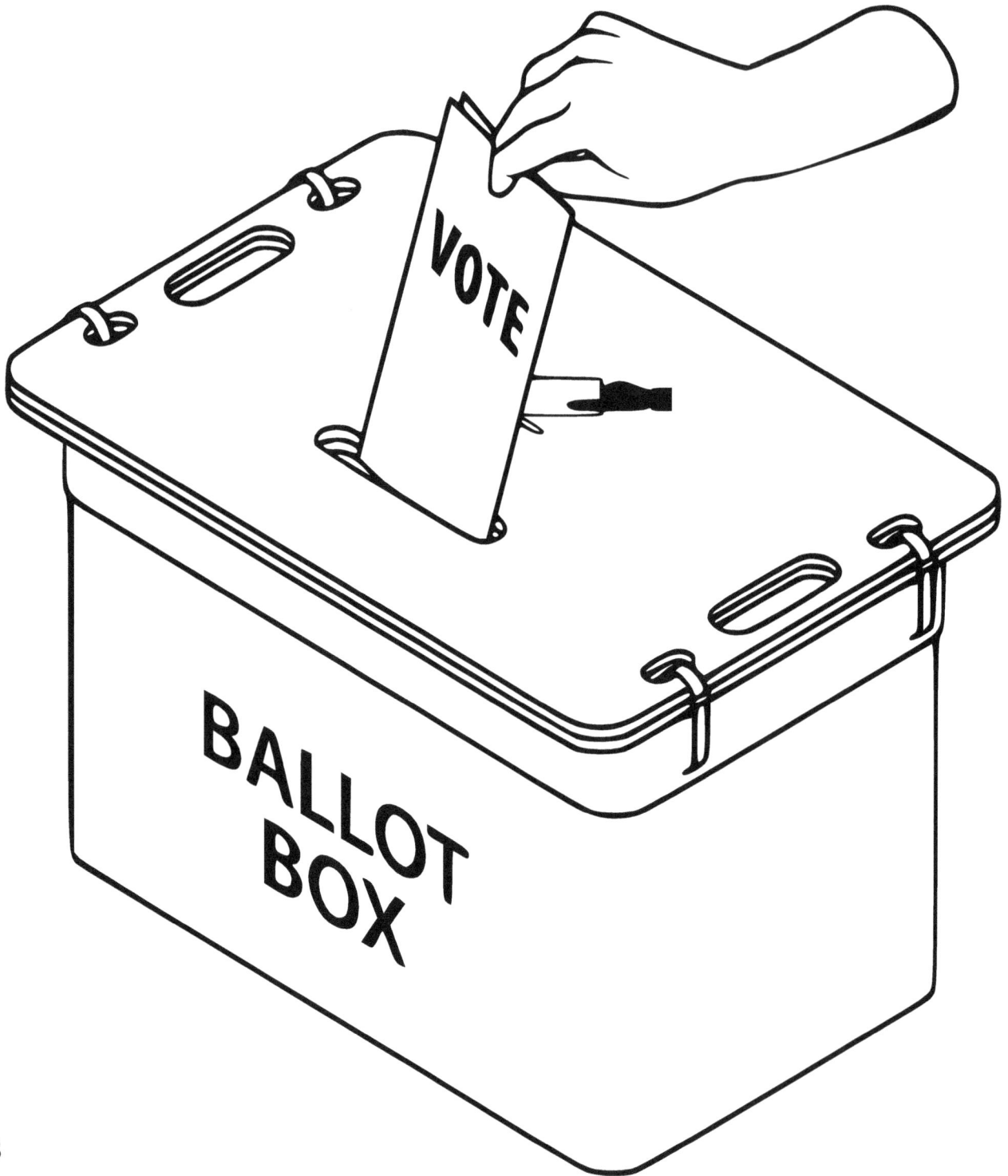

VOTE

BALLOT
BOX

VOTE DEMOCRAT

24

VOTE

REPUBLICAN

Election Day

BALLOT
☑ Yes
☐ NO
Yes
☑ NO

BALLOT
BOX

30

I VOTED TODAY

Meet the Author

Meet Alisa Ladawn Grace, a retired school administrator, Chief Operating Officer of a nonprofit company, Transformation Life Coach, and a fervent advocate for children's civic education. Alisa has authored not one but three engaging and informative children's books focused on civics: "Civic Heroes: Discovering Elections with the Supervisor of Elections" (ages 6-9), "My Civic Adventure: Learning About Voting and Community!" (ages 3-5), and "Election Essentials with the Supervisor of Elections: A Guide to Civics for Young Citizens" (ages 10-13).

Recognizing the importance of early civic education, Alisa's books introduce children to fundamental concepts like democracy, voting rights, and the electoral process in an age-appropriate and enjoyable way. Her work aims to inspire the next generation of informed and responsible voters, empowering them to participate in their communities and actively shape a better future.

Alisa's belief in the potential of young minds is deeply rooted in her diverse experiences. From her career in education to her role as a Transformation Life Coach, she has seen firsthand the transformative power of guidance. Her passion for guiding individuals toward personal growth and spiritual fulfillment is a belief and a mission evident in her writing.

Alisa's practical guide, "Unlocking Your Great Potential Within You: The Supernatural Powers of Meditation, Executive Functioning Skills, and Good Habits for Kids 3-18 Years Old,"
Is not just a book but a toolkit for success and well-being.
It equips children with tools they can apply immediately,
 emphasizing the importance of faith, integrity, and love in an immediately applicable way.

Through her writing, Alisa seeks to make a positive difference in the lives of children and families, fostering a lifelong commitment to civic engagement and unlocking the great potential of every young citizen.

www.ingramcontent.com/pod-product-compliance
Lightning Source LLC
LaVergne TN
LVHW061331060426
835513LV00015B/1356